The
ANCIENT
WORLD
in 100 WORDS

Quarto is the authority on a wide range of topics.

Quarto educates, entertains and enriches the lives of our readers—enthusiasts and lovers of hands-on living.

www.quartoknows.com

Author: Clive Gifford
Illustrator: Gosia Herba
Designer: Victoria Kimonidou
Editor: Harriet Stone
Editorial Director: Laura Knowles
Creative Director: Malena Stojic
Publisher: Maxime Boucknooghe

First published in 2019 by words & pictures,
an imprint of The Quarto Group.
26391 Crown Valley Parkway, Suite 220
Mission Viejo, CA 9269
T: +1 949 380 7510
F: +1 949 380 7575
www.QuartoKnows.com

A CIP record for this book is available from the Library of Congress.

ISBN 978 0 7112 4466 5

Manufactured in Shenzhen, China PP082019

9 8 7 6 5 4 3 2 1

The ANCIENT WORLD in 100 WORDS

Words by **CLIVE GIFFORD**
Pictures by **GOSIA HERBA**

words & pictures

CONTENTS

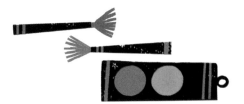

Egyptians
Around 3500 BCE–30 BCE
Based around the Nile, this civilization brought us pharaohs, pyramids, tombs, and treasures.

Phoenicians
Around 2500 BCE–300 BCE
Sailors and traders extended the Phoenicians' influence across the Mediterranean.

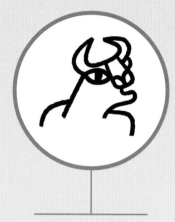

Minoans
Around 2700 BCE–1200 BCE
The first advanced civilization in Europe was centered on the island of Crete and reached its peak in the period 1900–1400 BCE.

Look out for the symbols on each page. They show which ancient civilization the 100-word entry relates to. Some entries relate to more than one civilization.

Pharaohs

Kings reigned over Egypt from about 3100 until 30BCE. They were later called pharaohs, from the word *per-aa*, meaning "great house"—the palaces they lived in. A pharaoh had ultimate power over Egypt, being in charge of the government and laws. They built temples and took part in religious ceremonies to keep the gods on their side. Dead pharaohs were given elaborate funerals and grand tombs to ensure their spirits joined the gods. Pharaohs were often shown wearing a beard, which was usually false, and holding a crook called a *heka*—a symbol of them as shepherd of Egypt's people.

Amulet

Ancient civilizations were very superstitious. Many people looked to gain good luck and protect themselves against evil by wearing charms known as amulets. Ancient Egyptians often chose green-blue amulets in the shape of a particular god or the Eye of Horus, as the colors represented life and good health. They also thought their dead needed protection, so many amulets were put in tombs. In ancient Rome, baby boys were given a *bulla*—an amulet on a necklace made of lead or gold which they wore until adulthood. Other Romans carried amulets in pouches around their waist, to ward off evil.

Greeks

Around 800 BCE–146 BCE

Ancient Greece was at its peak between these years, pioneering ideas, arts, and sciences, though their influence extended before and after.

Romans

753 BCE–476 CE

Expert conquerors and masters of organization, the Romans dominated the ancient world at its peak.

INTRODUCTION

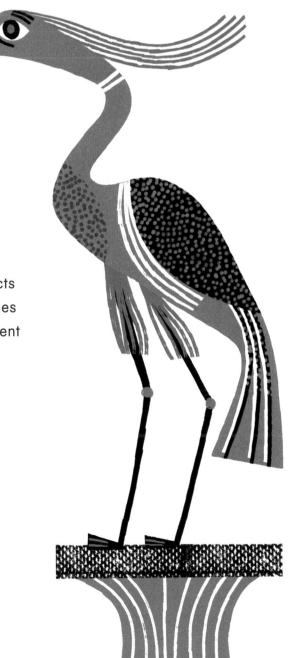

The land around the Mediterranean Sea was home to a number of extraordinary ancient civilizations, beginning with the **Egyptians** more than 5,000 years ago. In the space of 3,500 years, the Egyptians, **Greeks** and **Romans**, as well as the **Minoans** and **Phoenicians**, developed, battled, and flourished. These civilizations were eventually wiped out or faded away, but they left behind a treasure trove of objects and stunning buildings from the towering pyramids and creepy mummies of ancient Egypt, to the ideas, art, theater, and Olympic games of ancient Greece, and the roads, aqueducts, and laws of the ancient Romans.

This book takes on the challenge of summing up the ancient world in just 100 words. Each word reflects an important place, character, idea, invention, or event from the time. They've been chosen carefully to give you a thorough idea of what the ancient world was like. Each entry will also make you think and spark discussions with others.

Are you ready to adventure into the amazing ancient world? Just turn the page...

Nile

Running more than 4,100 miles through Africa and emptying into the
Mediterranean Sea, the River Nile dominated ancient Egypt. Most Egyptian people lived
nearby, benefiting from its annual floods which enriched the soil with nutrients, and channeling
its waters into reservoirs to be used during the dry seasons. The Nile was the main transport and
trade route through Egypt, with barges and boats made of woven reeds traveling its length.
The river also proved a rich source of food, with fish such as mullet, carp, catfish and perch,
as well as duck, geese, and crane birds, often caught using nets.

Mummies

Preserving the body of a dead person or animal in ancient Egypt
was called mummification. Making a mummy took around 70 days. The body was
packed with natron salt to dry it out. The stomach, lungs, intestines, and liver were removed
and stored in four canopic jars, but the heart was left in place to guide the person through
the afterlife. The brain was thought unimportant and pulled out through the nostrils and
thrown away. After washing and covering in resin, the body was wrapped in linen bandages
with amulets—good luck charms—laid in between the layers before burial.

Pharaohs

Kings reigned over Egypt from about 3100 until 30BCE. They were later called
pharaohs, from the word *per-aa*, meaning "great house"—the palaces they lived in. A pharaoh
had ultimate power over Egypt, being in charge of the government and laws. They built
temples and took part in religious ceremonies to keep the gods on their side. Dead pharaohs
were given elaborate funerals and grand tombs to ensure their spirits joined the gods.
Pharaohs were often shown wearing a beard, which was usually false, and holding
a crook called a *heka*—a symbol of them as shepherd of Egypt's people.

Amulet

Ancient civilizations were very superstitious. Many people looked to gain
good luck and protect themselves against evil by wearing charms known as amulets.
Ancient Egyptians often chose green-blue amulets in the shape of a particular god or
the Eye of Horus, as the colors represented life and good health. They also thought their dead
needed protection, so many amulets were put in tombs. In ancient Rome, baby boys were given
a *bulla*—an amulet on a necklace made of lead or gold which they wore until adulthood.
Other Romans carried amulets in pouches around their waist, to ward off evil.

Scribes

A highly prized job in ancient Egypt, scribes were vital for running the country
—from collecting taxes and recording harvests of crops, to copying out religious writings.
Some adventurous scribes traveled with Egypt's armies, writing reports and ordering supplies.
A scribe's many years of training began at age eight or nine. They learned to read and write
the more than 700 symbols that made up hieroglyphs as well as a simpler writing system
called hieratic. Scribes prayed to their own god, Thoth, for success in their work and
some scribes managed to rise to become viziers—advisers to the pharaoh.

Sphinx

This mythical creature with the head of a human and the body of a lion
was actually named by the ancient Greeks, but the most famous sphinx of all is
undoubtedly Egyptian. Carved out of limestone rock over 4,500 years ago, the Great Sphinx
is one of the biggest and oldest surviving monuments in the world. It is truly enormous,
measuring 234 feet long and 66 feet tall, and sits close to the Great Pyramid
at Giza. Erosion and vandalism means the Great Sphinx has lost its beard,
nose, and bright paint, but this does not detract from its grandeur.

Osiris

Ancient Egyptians believed that a dead person's soul traveled to
the afterlife, where it faced certain tests. Osiris was a powerful Egyptian god
who tested each soul and was in charge of the afterlife. If the person's soul was judged
worthy enough, then it was turned into a shining spirit called an *akh*. According to myths,
Osiris was the first king of Egypt and both the brother and husband of the goddess Isis.
He was often shown in paintings as a mummified Egyptian pharaoh with green skin,
which shows his other roles of god of fertility and god of farming.

Hieroglyphs

Hieroglyphs formed ancient Egypt's most famous writing system. Examples are found etched on temple columns, pressed into clay tablets, and inked on papyrus scrolls from as far back as 5,200 years ago. More than 700 hieroglyph symbols existed, each representing different sounds or words. A rectangle with a gap, for example, meant "house," while a mouth shape could mean "mouth," "spell," or the sound of a letter "r." Confusingly, a message in hieroglyphs could be written vertically, horizontally, from left to right, or right to left. A pharaoh's name was sometimes written using hieroglyphs inside an oval, called a cartouche.

Cubit

· ·

If you measure from the tip of an adult's middle finger to their elbow, that distance (17-21 inches) is a cubit. Invented in Egypt around 3000 BCE, this was one of the first widely used measurements in the ancient world. Teams of rope-stretchers used 12-cubit-long ropes to re-mark Egyptian farm fields after floods from the river washed their boundaries away. A 20.6-inch-long Royal Cubit made of granite rock was used as a standard in ancient Egypt for other cubit rods to be made out of wood. One cubit rod was found in the tomb of Maya, treasurer to the pharaoh Tutankhamun.

Pets

Can you imagine having a baboon as a pet? What about a hippo or a lion?
Some ancient Egyptians kept these creatures, as well as hawks, ibises, and even crocodiles.
Cats, though, were sacred. Known as *miu* or *miut* (he or she that mews), they killed snakes
and mice and were associated with Bastet, the Egyptian goddess of childbirth and the home.
Pet cats were sometimes mummified or buried as offerings to the gods. Some households
shaved their eyebrows in grief when their favorite cat died. In 1888, some ancient
Egyptian tombs were found to hold around 80,000 mummified cats.

Pyramids

These giant marvels of construction were built as tombs for many ancient Egyptian pharaohs and their families. The first pyramid was built for pharaoh Djoser at the Saqqara burial ground, 4,600 years ago. Over 110 ancient pyramids have been found in Egypt. The grandest of all—the Great Pyramid at Giza—was made for the pharaoh Khufu and stood 479 feet tall (the world's tallest building for 3,800 years). Built from 2.3 million giant limestone blocks, the pyramid weighs the same as a million elephants! Later pharaohs, such as Tutankhamun, were buried underground in tombs cut into the rocky landscape.

Shabtis

Ancient Egyptians were often buried with these 4–20-inch models of people.
At first, they were designed to act as a spare body for the person being buried, in case
something went wrong with their mummified body. Later on, the numbers of Shabtis in tombs
grew. These figures often held tools such as hoes and seed bags, showing that they were servants
who would work for the dead person in the afterlife. The wealthier you were, the more shabtis
you might buy from temples to be buried with. The pharaoh Tutankhamun's tomb
contained 413 shabtis along with 1,866 model tools.

Beer

Ancient Egyptians—from pharaohs to peasants—drank beer, and lots of it.
According to records unearthed by archaeologists, workers helping to build
the pyramids at Giza were each given about a gallon of beer per day! Ancient Egyptian
beer was unlike what we have today. It was usually thick, sometimes lumpy, and made with
barley or by crumbling bread into water and leaving it to ferment in jars. The drink might
be sweetened by adding dates or figs during the brewing process. The end result
was a quick source of energy that was drunk by children as well as adults.

Hatshepsut

The queen who dared to be king, Hatshepsut (around 1507–1458BCE) declared herself
ruler of Egypt after her husband, Thutmose II, died and her son, Thutmose III, was too young
to govern. Over a 22-year reign, she proved a smart leader, repairing old temples and building
grand new ones to keep in with Egypt's powerful priests. She wore the ceremonial clothes and
false beard of male pharaohs and used propaganda to show off her successes. She also
re-opened trade routes and sponsored expeditions by ships traveling south into Africa,
which brought back riches including gold, myrrh trees, spices, and fragrances.

Corvée

Most ancient Egyptians lacked hard cash. Banknotes hadn't been invented, and coins didn't arrive until near the end of the civilization. Instead, people exchanged goods or their work and skills. Rather than paying tax with money, people worked for free for the kingdom, often for several months per year. This was called corvée. Outside the farming season many people worked on large building projects such as canals, temples, or new cities. In the past, historians thought the Great Pyramid and other tombs were built by slaves, but they now believe that many of the workers were people performing their corvée.

Vizier

· ·

After the pharaoh, the single most powerful person in ancient Egypt was the vizier. The pharaoh's most trusted adviser, the vizier was in charge of running the country— from collecting taxes to organizing grand building projects. Nearly all were men—the first female vizier, Nebet, was adviser to her son-in-law, Pepi I. Some viziers survived a change of pharaoh. Hori, for example, served as vizier to five different rulers of Egypt. Other viziers got the top job when a pharaoh died and left no heir to take over. Paramessu, vizier to Horemheb, became pharaoh Ramesses I around 3,310 years ago.

Papyrus

Our word "paper" comes from this ancient Egyptian writing material first produced over 5,000 years ago and later used by the Greeks and Romans. It was made from flattened strips of marsh reeds which grew around the River Nile. The reed strips were beaten flat, laid in a criss-crossing pattern, and dried under a heavy weight. Some papyrus scrolls, such as the Ebers Papyrus, were around 66 feet long. Ancient Egyptian scribes would write or paint on papyrus using a brush made from frayed reeds, dipped in ink created from soot or ground down minerals mixed with water or oil.

Hittites

Around 3,600 years ago, a new empire began forming, centered in what is now Turkey and northern Syria. The Hittites were one of the first peoples to work iron and to use fast-moving chariots in battle to shock and awe the enemy. They scored many notable victories against rivals, including ancient Egypt. The biggest known battle between the two foes was at Kadesh in 1274 BCE, which involved over 5,000 chariots and as many as 70,000 foot soldiers. It failed to end with a clear victor and 16 years later the two sides signed the first recorded peace treaty in history.

Tutankhamun

Ancient Egyptian pharaoh Tutankhamun died in 1327 BCE, aged just 18. His fame
comes from the discovery of his tomb in 1922 by British archaeologist Howard Carter.
Unlike most royal tombs which had already been robbed, his was completely intact and packed
full of incredible riches. Over 5,000 objects (many now on display in a museum in Cairo) were
buried with the teenage pharaoh, including a golden chariot, 130 walking sticks, furniture,
statues, and 40 pairs of sandals. His mummified body was found inside a nest of three
coffins, the inner one made of more than 240 pounds of solid gold.

Cosmetics

Makeup is not a modern invention. Ancient Egyptian women and men wore elaborate eye makeup of green paint and thick black kohl eyeliner made from fat, soot, and crushed metals and rocks. Berries, red ants, and red clay would be ground up with shiny fish scales to make lipstick. Wealthy Greek women would mix charcoal with olive oil to make eye shadow and would redden their cheeks using beetroot. In most ancient civilizations, people prized pale skin, so face-whitening powders were created. However, many of these contained poisonous powdered lead, and one Roman recipe included donkey's milk and crocodile dung!

Ra

One of ancient Egypt's oldest and most important gods, Ra was also
known as Re or Pra. The god of the Sun or creation, Ra was often shown with
the head of a falcon surrounded by a large disc to represent the Sun. The earliest
drawings of Ra are more than 4,500 years old. Some myths said that humans were
created from his tears, and ancient Egyptians believed that Ra traveled across the
sky each day in a boat known as a solar barque. As night fell, he was eaten
by Nut, the sky goddess, but was reborn each morning.

Ramesses II

The only pharaoh to ever be issued a passport, Ramesses II's
3,200-year-old mummy was flown to Paris in 1974 for preservation work. He was
given a welcome fit for a king! In ancient Egypt, most people died before age 40, but
Ramesses lived to be around 90 years old. He ruled for 67 years and had at least 90 children.
He led many battles in Syria accompanied by his pet lion and started an incredible
period of building throughout Egypt. Temples were cut into rock faces at Abu Simbel
and a new capital city was built, named Pi-Ramesses after himself.

Nilometer

The Nile governed the seasons for farmers in ancient Egypt, with the river flooding its banks from June onward. How much and how quickly the river flooded could be the difference between farming failure and success. Nilometers were columns sunk into the river bed or large stone staircases descending down into the river. Officials monitored these as flooding began and could predict the speed and likely size of that year's flood. If the flood was too high, it might wash away fields and dams. If it was too low, there may not be enough water to ensure a good harvest.

Horus

This falcon-headed Egyptian god of the sky was the son of Osiris and Isis.
He is said to have lost an eye while fighting the god of chaos and storms, Set (or Seth).
The eye was repaired by the god Thoth, and the Eye of Horus, or *Wedjat*, became a
popular good luck charm and symbol of healing. The spirit of Horus was said to enter
each Egyptian ruler when they were crowned pharaoh, making them gods on Earth.
Horus's four sons—Qebehsenuef, Hapy, Imsety, and Duamutef—protected
the body parts stored in canopic jars when a person was mummified.

Rosetta

· ·

When a 1,676-pound chunk of rock carved with symbols was found in the Egyptian
town of Rosetta, it proved to be the key to unlocking the mystery of Egyptian hieroglyphs
and their meaning. The stone was discovered in 1799 by a French soldier. What made it
priceless was that its message—an announcement from the pharaoh Ptolemy V—was written
not only in hieroglyphs, but also in ancient Greek. This allowed scientists and historians, most
notably French scholar Jean-François Champollion, to work out hieroglyphs' meaning
by the 1820s. The stone now sits on display in the British Museum in London.

Cleopatra

One of the ancient world's most fascinating and intriguing figures, Cleopatra was the last pharaoh of an independent Egypt. Highly educated and able to speak many languages, she came to power in 51 BCE at the age of 18 and sought the help of Roman leaders to stay in charge. She later married Roman general Marc Antony and the pair led warships into battle against the Romans at the Battle of Actium in 31 BCE. They suffered a crushing defeat and fled back to Alexandria where, in 30 BCE, Cleopatra took her own life, after which Egypt became part of the Roman Empire.

Phoenicians

More than 4,000 years ago, the Phoenicians lived on a narrow strip of land in Asia
bordering the eastern Mediterranean Sea. With their land surrounded by high mountains,
they looked to expand outward by sea, becoming the ancient world's most skilled shipbuilders,
sailors, and traders. Reaching a peak between 1200 and 800 BCE, the Phoenicians traveled throughout
the Mediterranean using wide *gauloi* ships to trade with other civilizations, especially the Greeks
and Egyptians. They built towns and cities in North Africa and Turkey and are also believed
to have sailed out into the Atlantic Ocean, possibly reaching Ireland and Great Britain.

Purple

Until the invention of artificial dyes 150 years ago, all coloring for clothes
came from nature, with purple dyes being the rarest and most prized. The strongest,
longest-lasting purple dye came from the slime of tiny murex sea snails, which the
Phoenicians harvested from the port of Tyre. It took more than 9,000 snails to make a single
gram of dye. As a result, Tyrian purple was phenomenally expensive—at times, more than
three times the price of gold. During long periods of the Roman Empire, only emperors
and statues of Roman gods were permitted to wear Tyrian purple clothing.

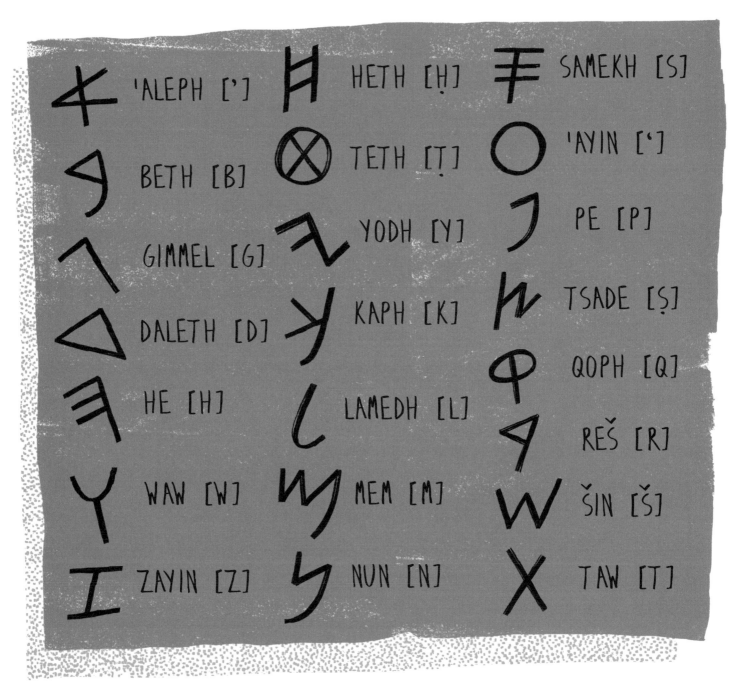

'ALEPH [']

BETH [B]

GIMMEL [G]

DALETH [D]

HE [H]

WAW [W]

ZAYIN [Z]

HETH [Ḥ]

TETH [Ṭ]

YODH [Y]

KAPH [K]

LAMEDH [L]

MEM [M]

NUN [N]

SAMEKH [S]

'AYIN [']

PE [P]

TSADE [Ṣ]

QOPH [Q]

REŠ [R]

ŠIN [Š]

TAW [T]

Alphabet

When early people wrote, they used pictures or symbols to represent different objects, ideas, and actions. This meant they had to learn hundreds of different symbols to be able to write. Around 3,500 years ago, the Phoenicians figured out that most words were made up of just a small number of simple sounds. They constructed an alphabet containing just 22 symbols, each representing one of these sounds. Used together, these could spell out words. As traders and sailors, the Phoenicians traveled widely, carrying their new alphabet around the ancient world. It inspired the creation of the Greek and other alphabets.

Byblos

One of the world's oldest cities, people have lived in Byblos for over 7,000 years. Also known as Gebal, it grew under Phoenician rule, from a fishing village to a wealthy trading center. Its location, on the eastern edge of the Mediterranean Sea, made it the perfect place for trading between Cyprus, Egypt, and Greece. Ships left Byblos carrying grapes, slaves, cloth, and timber from stout cedar trees that grew nearby. All sorts of goods were bought and sold, but the trade for papyrus, used for writing, was so huge that the ancient Greeks named books *biblion* after the city.

Minoans

Mediterranean Europe's first major civilization flourished on the island of Crete from 2700 BCE for around 1,500 years. The Minoans built elaborate palaces surrounded by workshops and houses at a number of locations on Crete—the largest is found at Knossos. They were also skilled pottery makers and metalworkers, and their beautiful frescoes—paintings made directly onto wet plaster on walls—give archaeologists clues about how they lived. We believe that Minoan men wore a sort of kilt over a loincloth, while women wore colorful dresses. The Minoans were good sailors who traded with Egypt and other places around the Mediterranean.

Knossos

The ancient Minoans built a number of impressive palaces around 3,500–4,000 years ago.
The grandest was Knossos. Covering an area larger than two football fields, this stone
palace complex had flat wooden roofs, a maze of corridors (which may have inspired the
Greek myth of the minotaur in the labyrinth), and elaborate decorations inside. Many decorations
featured bulls, an animal that was sacred to Minoans. Ancient paintings at Knossos show
the extremely dangerous tradition of "bull leaping." This is where teams of people took
turns to grab the horns of a charging bull and spring over the creature's back.

Minotaur

One of the most famous Greek myths is about this terrifying beast.
The Minotaur was said to eat human flesh, have the head and tail of a bull and
the body of a man. King Minos of Crete had a gigantic underground maze, called
a labyrinth, built to house the Minotaur. Every nine years 14 young men and women
were sent inside for the Minotaur to eat. According to legend, Theseus, the
King of Athens' son, volunteered to be one of the victims, but he managed
to slay the Minotaur, using a trail of string to find his way out.

Democracy

Democracy (meaning "rule by the people") first began in ancient Greece around 2,500 years ago. Before then, most city-states were ruled by one person, known as a tyrant. The citizens could not vote and had no power to change things in their city-state. In 508BCE, Athenian leader Cleisthenes introduced a new system of government where all male citizens (but not women, slaves, or non-Athenian Greeks) got their own say on how the city-state was run. Each citizen could speak and vote at 40 meetings a year, known as the Assembly, before new laws were put into action by the Council.

Athens

Named after Athena, the Greek goddess of wisdom and warfare, Athens waged frequent wars against rival city-states and kingdoms, but was also a rich center of learning and the arts. It was built around a rocky outcrop (the Acropolis) and controlled the surrounding countryside known as Attica and an important port, Piraeus. At its peak, around 2,500 years ago, Athens could claim to be the most important city in the world. Many artists, writers, and thinkers, including Socrates and Plato, lived and worked in its crowded city streets overlooked by the Acropolis, where the city's most important temples were located.

Hades

Hades, the brother of Zeus and Poseidon, was god of the underworld—the place ancient Greeks, and later, Romans, believed people went when they died. He was often shown alongside Cerberus, a three-headed dog who guarded the gates of the underworld to prevent the living from entering and the dead from leaving. Over time, the god became known as Plouton or Pluto and the place he ruled over became known as Hades. It contained different areas, including the beautiful, sunlit Elysian Fields, where the souls of heroes and people who had lived good lives enjoyed the rest of their days.

Olives

The humble olive may not look like much, but it powered trade throughout the ancient world. Early olive farming began with the Minoans on Crete, before Phoenicians, Greeks, and Romans spread them throughout the Mediterranean. Olives were squashed with the feet, or later with mechanical presses, to produce oil, which was transported and traded in twin-handled jars called *amphorae*. It was used in food, cooking, massage, as fuel for lamps, and in religious ceremonies. It was also used as soap and a medicine. The famous Greek doctor Hippocrates listed more than 60 ailments that could be treated with olive oil.

Coins

Before coins, people would swap or barter goods and services. The oldest known
coins were minted in Lydia (a kingdom within present-day Turkey), 2,600 years ago.
These were round or bean-shaped objects made of electrum—a mixture of gold and silver.
They were fashioned with different designs including deer, lions, and even a seal eating an octopus.
Within decades, coins caught on in ancient Greece, most being made of pure silver or gold.
From 510 CE onward, silver tetradrachm coins from Athens, with an owl on one side
and the goddess Athena on the other, were widely used throughout ancient Greece.

Olympics

First held in 776BCE, and continuing once every four years for over 1,000 years,
this Greek festival in honor of the god Zeus grew to be the ancient world's biggest
sporting event. A truce was made before each games, allowing safe travel to Olympia for
the more than 50,000 spectators and athletes. Over time, competitions came to include
horse racing, boxing, and a pentathlon. Competitors were all male—married women weren't
even allowed to watch! Olympic champions received crowns of olive leaves, called *kotinos*,
as prizes, but back home they could be rewarded with houses or free meals for life.

Pankration

Of all the ancient Olympic sports, pankration (meaning "all force") was the most brutal and the most popular with spectators. Added to the games in 648 BCE, this combination of wrestling and boxing without gloves had almost no rules—only biting and eye gouging were outlawed. Strangling, punching, kicking, and choking were all acceptable and bouts continued until one competitor gave up or became unconscious. Pankration champions showed no mercy. Sostratos of Sicyon, for instance, was a three-time champion in 364, 360, and 356 BCE. He was said to break the fingers of his opponent, one by one, until they admitted defeat.

Stadion

The only race at the first 13 ancient Olympic games, the stadion is where we get the word stadium from. The sprint was held on a 623-foot-long stretch of ground and featured up to 20 men, all naked and barefoot. Woe betide you if you made a false start as officials might punish you with a public flogging using whips. Coroebus, a baker from the Greek city-state of Elis, became the very first Olympic champion when he won the stadion race in 776 BCE. Later games featured a two-stadion-long *diaulos* race and a grueling run wearing soldier's armor called a *dolichos*.

Oracle

Ancient Greeks liked to consult their gods before they started any important tasks. Many would go to see an oracle for advice. Oracles were priests or priestesses who were thought to be able to speak directly with ancient Greek gods. The messages they received were also known as oracles. The most famous oracle was at Delphi. There, one or more priestesses, each known as a *Pythia*, were believed to communicate with the Greek god of prophecy and truth, named Apollo. People would travel from all over the Greek world to wait at Delphi and receive a message from the god.

Salamis

In 480 BCE, the island of Salamis, just 10 miles from Athens, bore witness
to one of the first major naval battles in history. Xerxes' Persian navy of nearly 1,000 fighting
vessels vastly outnumbered the 370 Greek ships. Yet, the Greek commander, Themistocles,
had a cunning plan and lured the Persians into the narrow waters between Salamis and the
Greek mainland. With no room to maneuver, around 300 Persian ships were sunk, mostly by
Greek triremes making holes in their hulls with giant battering rams. The Greeks scored
a resounding victory, losing only 40 ships and stopping Xerxes from conquering Athens.

Asklepios

This Greek god of healing was believed to possess miraculous medical powers. We get the word hygiene from his daughter, Hygieia, goddess of cleanliness. Asklepios was often shown holding a staff with a snake wound around it. Ill or injured Greeks would flock to healing temples called *Asklepeions*. There, they might stay overnight, hoping to be healed as they slept or be given herbal remedies by the temple's priests. Visitors often left clay models of the body parts that had caused them problems as an offering of thanks to Asklepios. The ancient Romans adopted the god, and renamed him Asclepius.

Catapult

Wanting a weapon that packed more of a punch, the Greeks invented catapults around 400 BCE. They hurled arrows and spears greater distances than a soldier could throw them. Catapults quickly developed into different types of powerful weapons used by Greeks, Romans, and other forces. Onagers were capable of hurling rocks weighing up to 154 pounds with enough force to smash down walls or kill enemy soldiers. The ballista was like a giant crossbow using cords of rope or animal sinew twisted to build up power. When the cords were released, they could fire a weapon distances of over 1,310 feet.

Agora

This ancient Greek market was the center of life in most towns and cities. People would gather to exchange gossip, make plans, and buy and sell. Philosophers and politicians might wander through the crowds, trying to publicize their thoughts. Many agora contained a temple or statues and were lined by columned buildings called *stoa*, which contained many shops and stalls, selling everything from food and fabrics, to pottery and metalwork. Untrustworthy sellers, who tricked customers by using fake weights, feared the arrival of a *metronomoi*—a Greek official who ensured weights were accurate. Guilty traders could face fines or beatings.

Theater

Theaters first began with the ancient Greeks, who enjoyed plays performed on semi-circular stages called *orchestras* at the base of sloping hills called *theatron*, meaning "watching place." Open-air stone theaters were built later. The theaters at Argos and Ephesus are thought to have held audiences of 20,000. Theater-goers needed stamina, as some plays lasted all day. They were either comedies or tragedies and were performed by only male actors, often using character masks. In 493 BCE, one playwright, Phrynichus, was fined a huge sum of money—twice a farmer's yearly pay—for writing a play so sad that the audience cried.

Parthenon

Built between 447 and 438 BCE, when Athens was at its peak, this majestic temple was dedicated to the goddess Athena. It replaced a former temple destroyed by Persian invaders in 480 BCE. Athens spared no expense with its size and construction, making it mostly out of white marble. The temple cost 469 talents of silver to build; just one talent would buy an entire trireme, the most advanced warship at the time. Equal to 8¼ tennis courts in size, the Parthenon also acted as the city's treasury, became a Christian church in the sixth century CE, and later a Muslim mosque.

Sparta

This military-minded Greek city-state battled with Athens for supremacy in
the 5th century BCE. Ruled by two royal families and a council of five *ephors*, or overseers,
the state valued strength and fitness over arts and philosophy and was organized to produce
a very powerful army. At the age of seven, boys left home and began their *agoge*—military
training and education. Conditions were tough, food was sparse, and beatings were common.
At age 20 they became soldiers and were given land, which was farmed by helots
(captured slaves), to provide food for both the soldiers' families and the army.

Hoplites

Hoplites formed the backbone of ancient Greek armies. These armored foot soldiers fought in tight formations known as phalanxes, advancing close together so that the stout wooden shield of one hoplite also protected the soldier on his left. Each soldier wielded an 8 foot or longer spear tipped with bronze or iron, and kept a short sword known as a *xiphos* tucked into his belt. Bronze shin guards called greaves and a leather or bronze chest plate provided protection, as did helmets. These were often topped with a crest made of horse hair, making the soldiers look taller and fiercer.

Hercules

This celebrated mythical hero was adopted by the Romans from the Greek hero, Herakles. The son of a god and a human, many Romans identified with Hercules because he made mistakes and suffered just like ordinary people, but was also shown with godlike powers such as amazing strength and courage. These powers were put to the test when he had to perform 12 incredibly tough tasks, known as labors. Hercules completed all 12 labors, starting with strangling the mighty Nemean Lion with his bare hands and ending with him capturing Cerberus, the fearsome many-headed dog that guarded Hades, the underworld.

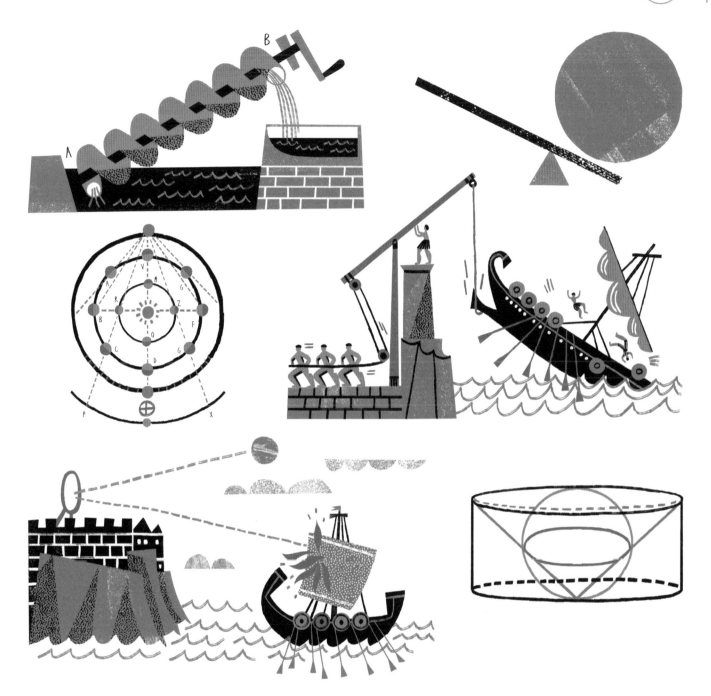

Archimedes

Born in Syracuse, Sicily, in 287 BCE and educated in Alexandria in Egypt, Archimedes made many advances in math, science, and engineering. He learned how to calculate the volume of cylinders and spheres and showed how heavier loads could be lifted, either through increasing the length of levers or by combining pulleys. His many inventions included screw pumps to raise water from deep rivers and war machines to defend his beloved Syracuse. Because of his status, during the Roman invasion of Syracuse, Roman commander Marcellus gave orders to "spare the mathematician." The command was ignored, and Archimedes was killed in 212 BCE.

Alexander

You don't get called "the Great" without good reason and this Macedonian general achieved a lot during his brief life (356–323 BCE). The son of King Philip II of Macedonia, Alexander was born in 356 BCE and had Aristotle as his personal tutor. He became king at the age of 20, and in just ten years had built one of the biggest empires the ancient world had ever seen, stretching from Greece and Egypt, through the Middle East, Persia, and into part of India. Along the way he spread Greek culture and built more than 20 cities, including Alexandria in Egypt.

Zeus

The mightiest of the ancient Greek gods, Zeus was portrayed as their king and
lived in the clouds above Mount Olympus with his wife, Hera, the goddess of marriage
and love. As the god of the skies, Zeus was thought to control the stars, winds, and weather,
as well as upholding law and order. He was said to punish wrongdoers with lightning
and thunderbolts, often carried by Pegasus, a winged horse. Altars in the courtyards
of many Greek homes were dedicated to his worship, while the ancient Romans
had a very similar king of the gods, named Jupiter or Jove.

Socrates

Born around 470 BCE, Socrates served in Athens' army before becoming a full-time philosopher. He believed that "The unexamined life is not worth living." He used all of Athens as his classroom, teaching on the streets every day. His teaching method involved bombarding his students, including Plato, with many questions to reveal gaps in their knowledge. He encouraged people to think for themselves and not always follow what society believes. His views made him enemies and in 400 BCE, he was put on trial for corrupting his students' minds and sentenced to death. He died the following year, by drinking poisonous hemlock.

Troy

Located on the western tip of Turkey, Troy was a once prosperous city and the location of the famous Trojan Horse myth, set during the Trojan War 3,200 years ago. After ten years of attacking Troy unsuccessfully, Greek soldiers concocted a cunning plan. They built a giant wooden model of a horse and left it outside the gates of the city as they pretended to retreat. The Trojans hauled the horse inside Troy's walls, only to find it full of Greek soldiers, who opened the city gates and let the rest of the Greek troops inside to capture the city.

Citizen

Ancient Greece was made up of lots of independent city-states, which controlled
the countryside surrounding their center. Each state was called a *polis*. The people of
a *polis* were divided into free people and slaves who had no legal rights. In some city-states,
such as Athens, free people were divided into *metics* (foreigners or outsiders) and citizens.
Male citizens took part in government and could vote on important matters. They also had
to serve in the army and were expected to volunteer for juries in courts. Metics and
female citizens in most city-states could not vote and had few rights.

Plato

This great thinker served in Athens' army, before becoming a student of the
philosopher Socrates. After Socrates' execution in 399BCE, Plato traveled widely throughout
the ancient world, finally coming back to Athens to open the Academy in 387BCE. This school of
higher learning would last for three centuries and count Aristotle among its pupils. Plato wrote on
a variety of topics including philosophy, art, mathematics, and politics, often in the form of dialogues
—conversations between people and his former mentor, Socrates. Plato's *Republic*, a book on justice,
human behaviour, and the ideal government, has influenced the western world ever since.

Aphrodite

Aphrodite was the ancient Greek goddess of beauty, fertility, and love.
Her beauty caused both gods and men to fight over her, even after Zeus ordered her
to marry the fearsome, ugly god of blacksmiths, Hephaestus. Aphrodite is often shown with
Eros, a minor god of love that was later adopted by the Romans, who renamed him Cupid.
Aphrodite was worshiped at temples, particularly in Cyprus and Corinth. Her symbols
included roses and doves, as well as dolphins, perhaps reflecting the myth that she
was born out of the foam of the sea and rode ashore on a giant seashell.

Gymnasium

Many ancient Greek cities featured an open-air space surrounded by columned buildings where young men could get fit. The men would train for the Olympics or other sporting games held in places such as Corinth and Delphi. These spaces got their name from the Greek word for nudity—*gymnos*—as the athletes all practiced and trained naked. A trainer called a *paidotribe*, often a former athlete, might help wrestlers, runners, or discus throwers with their technique, while an *aleiptes* would massage the athletes' tired muscles with olive oil. Gymnasiums also trained brains with educational lectures and became popular meeting places.

Aristotle

Born in 384 BCE, Aristotle studied with the philosopher Plato from the age of 17.
In 335 BCE he established his own school, the Lyceum, and was personal tutor to
Alexander the Great. Aristotle is most famous for his investigations into science, philosophy,
and logic. In his 200 written works, he proposed exciting new ways of studying the world
—from dissecting animals to classifying living things using logic. Not all of his ideas proved
correct, such as his belief that the heart is the center of intelligence, but his work was
pioneering at the time and had great influence for centuries afterward.

Gorgon

You definitely would not want to meet one of these fearsome creatures from ancient Greek mythology. It was believed that just one steely look from a gorgon's large eyes could turn a human into stone forever. With their prominent, pointed teeth, sinister faces and long hair made up of living venomous snakes, these creatures were terrifying to look at. In one Greek myth, Perseus, a son of Zeus, beheaded the most famous gorgon called Medusa. Some ancient Greeks placed *Gorgoneion*—stone engravings of a gorgon's face— on doors, walls, or shields in the belief that it would keep evil away.

Hippocrates

Born on the Greek island of Kos around 460 BCE, this pioneering medical man
was one of the first to separate medicine from superstition. He dismissed ideas that
diseases were caused by gods or spirits. Instead, he saw health problems as faults with the
human body for which cures could be found in nature—a revolutionary thought at the time.
Hippocrates opened a medical school on Kos, where he encouraged students to examine
and question each patient carefully. He thought nothing odd in tasting and smelling
a patient's sweat, urine, or earwax in order to diagnose what was wrong with them.

Slaves

Slaves in the ancient world were captured, often during wartime, and bought and sold just like cattle, pottery, or other goods. Some slave traders followed behind armies and gathered slaves for sale at markets. Slaves had few rights and were often treated very badly. Many slaves were employed as unpaid servants in rich homes, but others performed a wide variety of jobs. The Romans admired Greek culture, so some educated Greek slaves were employed as tutors and teachers. In contrast, many slaves faced back-breaking work as miners, farm laborers, or *lecticarii*—slaves that carried wealthy Romans about town in carriages.

Trireme

Large, fast, and deadly, these wooden warships were up to 130 feet long. When traveling longer distances they used sails, but in battle they relied on oar power, and lots of it. Three banks of oars lined the ship's sides, 170 oars in total. A pair of larger oars at the rear steered the warship. A trireme's main weapon was its monstrous battering ram made of wood and bronze. In battle, a trireme would speed straight ahead and use its ram to puncture holes in the vulnerable parts of enemy ships, splintering their wooden sides and often sinking the vessel.

Ostraca

Modern paper didn't exist in ancient Rome, Greece, or Egypt, but pottery was common. Shards of old pottery, called ostraca, were the scrap paper of their day. People painted, wrote in ink, or scratched pictures, hieroglyphs, or letters on ostraca. They were also used by schoolchildren and scribes to practice writing. The citizens of Athens used ostraca to cast their votes when a person threatened the peace or stability of the city. If the person lost the vote, they were ostracized, meaning they had 10 days to leave Athens. They could not return for 10 years on pain of death.

Romulus

More than 3,000 years ago, tribes settled in the hills above the River Tiber,
an area that eventually became the mighty city of Rome. However, the Romans
created a far more interesting tale for the origins of their city, based on twin boys—
Romulus and Remus. According to legend, the twins were abandoned and drank
the milk of a she-wolf until they were rescued by a herdsman. As adults, the twins
argued over where they should build a new city. Romulus killed Remus to get
his way. He founded the city of Rome in 753 CE on top of Palatine Hill.

Aqueduct

The Romans engineered mighty systems called aqueducts, meaning "waterways"
in Latin, to carry fresh water to towns and cities. These systems relied on gravity to transport
water from higher ground, along a mixture of channels, tunnels, and magnificent arched bridges,
into large storage tanks in the cities called *castellum*. The Romans built thousands of miles
of aqueducts throughout their empire—from Spain to Syria. The city of Rome was supplied by
11 different aqueducts, some carrying water from up to 55 miles away. The Aqua Virgo,
built in 19 BCE, still supplies water to a number of Rome's famous fountains today.

Gladiator

Gladiators fought—often to the death—for the entertainment of bloodthirsty crowds at Roman games. Most were slaves or criminals, although some free men chose to become gladiators and Emperor Commodus liked to take part, too! Gladiators trained in a school called a *ludus*. Pairs of gladiators would battle using different weapons. A *retiarius*, for instance, had a forked spear trident and a net to trap opponents. Most fighters were men, but some fights featured female gladiators or wild animals. Death was a constant threat —the most a gladiator could hope for was to win enough fights to gain freedom.

Hypatia

The daughter of a philosopher, Hypatia was born in the Egyptian city of Alexandria sometime between 350 and 370 CE. At a time when women weren't educated in schools, she became one of the Roman world's most famous mathematicians and the first known female astronomer. Hypatia built her own astrolabes—devices to study the movements of stars and planets across the night sky—and taught astronomy and philosophy to many students in Alexandria. Caught up in a bitter political feud in the city, she was beaten to death by an angry mob in 415 CE, an act which shocked the Roman world.

Emperor

··

In 27 BCE, Octavian was made the first emperor (supreme ruler) of the Roman Empire.
Emperors could raise taxes, make new laws, and order huge monuments to their greatness.
This male-only role was a job for life, without elections or early retirements. This meant Romans
were stuck with their ruler, even if they were very unpopular or unfit to govern. This led to
lots of murder plots. About 40 emperors were killed between 27 and 476 CE. Some emperors,
such as Pertinax and Caligula, were murdered by members of the Praetorian Guard—
the group of trusted elite soldiers supposed to protect them.

Spartacus

Born in northern Greece, Spartacus was sold into slavery and sent to Capua in Italy where he was trained as a gladiator. In 73 BCE, he and at least 50 other gladiators managed to escape, stealing wagons of weapons and hiding out in the forests on Mount Vesuvius. After defeating several small Roman armies, word spread, and the group was joined by more rebellious slaves. At its peak, Spartacus commanded a rebel army of more than 70,000. He proved a smart leader, defeating the Romans in a number of attacks before he lost an important battle and was killed in 71 BCE.

Hannibal

Born in 247 BCE, Hannibal Barca was the military leader of ancient Carthage, in northern Africa. He led an attack on Spain and then surprised the Romans by marching his forces, including African elephants, over the mountains and into Italy. He spent 16 years defeating Roman armies there, but never quite reached Rome. At the Battle of Trasimene in 217 BCE, he hid his entire army in order to ambush the Romans, and the following year he wiped out a force of 70,000 Romans. Returning home to defend Carthage from Roman attack, Hannibal was finally defeated at the 202 BCE Battle of Zama.

Caesar

Born in 100BCE, Julius Caesar was a soldier and politician who became governor of Spain in 61BCE and of Gaul (France) two years later. A skilled general, he conquered the rest of Gaul and Belgica (Belgium) before returning to Rome in 49BCE where he seized power after a civil war. He passed many new laws, abolished taxes, changed the calendar, and established a police force, all without the approval of other politicians. In 44BCE, he was made dictator for life…but this only lasted a few weeks as a group of politicians killed Caesar, which sparked off further civil wars.

Pozzolana

No ancient civilization used concrete as much as the Romans. Their Roman concrete, also called *opus caementicium*, contained a magic ingredient—volcanic ash called pozzolana. This helped make their concrete strong, water resistant, and extremely long-lasting. It even set well in water, making it ideal for harbors and underwater foundations. The Romans went concrete crazy, using it in roads, for the frames of buildings which were then covered in stone, and for molding into magnificent arches and domes. The Pantheon's 141-foot-wide dome was built in Rome 1,900 years ago. It is still the largest unsupported concrete dome in the world.

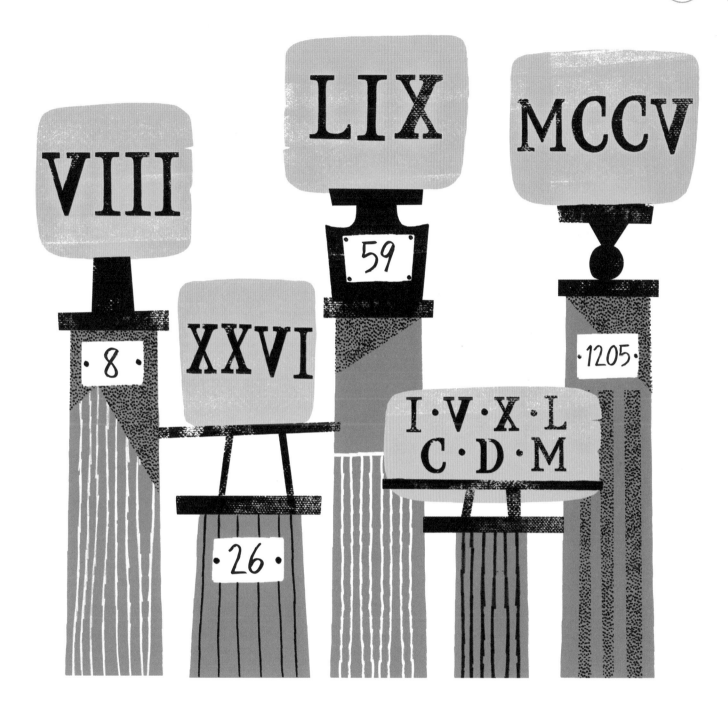

Numerals

Thousands of years ago, shepherds in southern Europe made little cuts
into sticks to keep track of the numbers in their herd. It is thought that the Romans'
number system came from this idea. The system used letters to represent numbers:
I=1, V=5, X=10, L=50, C=100, and M=1000. Although very logical, one disadvantage was that lots
of letters were needed to write some numbers. For example, "38" needed seven letters (XXXVIII).
Numerals continued to be used in Europe for centuries after Rome fell. They are still
found today on some clocks, monuments, and in the names of kings and queens.

Colosseum

Welcome to the greatest show on Earth! The Colosseum was a massive open-air amphitheater in the center of Rome, completed in 80ce. Measuring 620 by 512 feet, its limestone arches towered above the ground and were held in place by 330 tons of iron clamps. Around 50,000 spectators would arrive through the amphitheater's 80 entrances to watch executions, circus acts, and bloody contests between gladiators or wild animals. Lions, rhinoceros, elephants, and other creatures would be released from cages or the Colosseum's 36 trap doors. The arena was even occasionally flooded so that spectators could be entertained with naval battles.

Augustus

Rome's first emperor was born Gaius Octavius in 63 BCE and was adopted by his great uncle, Julius Caesar. When Caesar was killed in 44 BCE, Octavius vowed to avenge the murder and took part in a power struggle that ended with him becoming ruler of Rome in 31 BCE and then emperor in 27 BCE. Taking the name Augustus, he improved laws, established a postal service, expanded the roads, and transformed Rome with magnificent new buildings. During his 45-year reign, the empire nearly doubled in size and a period with few wars and great wealth began, known as the *Pax Romana* (Roman peace).

Grammaticus

These "schools" attended by Roman boys, especially those from rich families, were often just a room at the back of a shop, rented out by the teacher. The school day started at dawn with students studying oratory (public speaking), reading, literature, and poetry. Sometimes they were also taught mathematics, astronomy, history, and music. Roman schools had no gold stars or detentions—instead naughty students might be held down by a slave and whipped by a teacher. Roman girls only attended school until the age of ten. They would then have to stay at home, while boys carried on their education.

Toga

Think of ancient Roman clothing and chances are you'll think of the toga. These
large, roughly semi-circular pieces of thick woollen cloth had to be wrapped, folded, and
draped around the body. They could be heavy and awkward to wear, and unbearably hot in
summer. Apart from dark *toga pulla* worn at funerals, togas were white and got dirty quickly.
This meant a visit to the local cleaners, called a fullers, where people would trample on togas
and other garments soaked in a mixture of water and human and animal urine.
Ammonia in the urine helped clean stains from clothing.

Insula

Only wealthy Romans lived in countryside villas or in *domūs*—grand townhouses with courtyards. For most city dwellers, home was far less luxurious, often being in small, cramped apartment blocks called *insulae*. These were usually five floors high, although some may have reached up to nine floors, with the cheapest homes at the top. Most *insulae* didn't have a place to cook or running water, and waste had to be thrown out of the window onto the street below. Many *insulae* were cheaply built, using mud bricks and wood, so parts of these buildings often fell down or caught fire.

Mosaic

· ·

These exquisite artworks made of tiny tiles called *tesserae* first emerged in
ancient Greece around 2,400 years ago. The tiles were made of glass, stone, or pottery
and could be just millimeters in size. Mosaic artists would build up detailed pictures, usually on
floors, tile by tile. Mosaics became popular in Roman villas and palaces. The Villa Romana del
Casale in Sicily had mosaic floors that originally covered an area bigger than 14 tennis courts.
The famous Alexander mosaic in Pompeii, which shows Alexander the Great in battle
against the Persians, was made up of more than 1.5 million tiles.

Hypocausts

The Romans were epic innovators, as this central heating invention proves.
Taking its name from the Greek words for "under" and "burnt," hypocausts featured a furnace and a floor supported by pillars leaving an open space below. Slaves kept a fire burning fiercely in the furnace, producing hot air which circulated and heated rooms from below. Some hot air was directed up through channels in the walls to increase warmth. Although expensive to build and run, hypocausts were used in Roman baths, villas, and wealthy homes. After the Romans, home central heating in Europe did not return for 1,400 years.

Roads

Many ancient peoples built simple roads and trackways, but the Romans took it further. Using layers of packed soil, gravel, and cement topped with large paving stones, the Romans engineered hardwearing roads that stood the test of time. Without the use of machines, more than 50,000 miles of roads were constructed throughout the empire, some of which survive to this day. The roads were as straight as possible, allowing marching soldiers and traders to reach their destinations quickly. Most had a camber—a curved surface which directed rainwater away from the middle of the road into ditches at the sides.

Legionary

Being a legionary in the Roman army was pretty much a job for life...if you survived. These elite foot soldiers served for up to 25 years before retiring and receiving land and money. They needed to be tough and strong as they had to carry heavy tools and supplies on their backs during fast marches, for up to 19 miles a day. Legionaries were usually armed with a *pilum* (javelin), a small dagger, and a *gladius*—a 2-foot-long sword held in the right hand. In their left hand, they carried a large shield made from wood, leather, and iron.

Centurion

Centurions were experienced, battle-hardened soldiers in command of a unit
of around 100 men in the Roman Army. They were recognizable by the horsehair crest
on the top of their helmet and their sword worn on their left-hand side. They organized troops
into strong formations in battle, such as the *testudo* (tortoise), where soldiers would overlap
their shields at the front and above, to protect the closely packed unit from attacks. Centurions
often chose a deputy called an *optio* to assist them. Centurions were responsible for their
soldiers' discipline and could order beatings, or worse if their troops did badly.

Liberti

Good news for some slaves in ancient Rome. Unlike those in ancient Egypt and Greece, they could be freed by their owners in an act called manumission. Freed men and women were known as Liberti. Some slaves who worked in paid jobs saved enough money to buy their freedom, while others were freed as a reward by their owners. The playwright Terence was a slave until his owner, Roman senator Terentius Lucanus, read his writings and was so impressed he freed him. Some Liberti went on to succeed in business, while former slave Callixtus became Bishop of Rome in 218 CE.

Baths

When most Romans took a bath, it was in public. Romans flocked to large,
cheap baths that contained rooms and pools of different temperatures. Some stayed there
all day, taking advantage of the exercise areas called *palaestra* or the courtyards and gardens.
The baths' hottest room was the *laconicum*, heated by furnaces stoked with wood by slaves.
Bathers might pay other slaves to guard their clothes or to give them a massage.
The Romans didn't have soap. Instead they rubbed olive oil over their bodies and
then scraped the oil and grime away with a curved blade called a *strigil*.

Garum

Many Romans developed a real taste for strong, pungent flavors.
Chief among them was garum, a stinking sauce made from fish guts. These were mixed with salt and left to rot in the hot sun for several months until the mixture started to bubble and a liquid formed. Giant garum factories in Spain, Portugal, and elsewhere produced thousands of gallons of the sauce to supply intense demand. A liter of the highest quality *garum sociorum* could sell for the price of 300 loaves of bread. Garum was also taken as a medicine to cure diarrhea, ulcers, and even dog bites.

Nero

Whether mad or bad, this infamous emperor of Rome was definitely dangerous to know. Among those he had killed were close advisers, his first wife, and his mother. Nero was born in 37 CE and became emperor at 16. He ruled fairly at first, with a particular interest in Greek culture and music, before turning murderous. In 64 CE, a fire devastated Rome. Nero blamed the Christians and had many tortured and killed, then took advantage of the destruction to build a gigantic palace for himself. His extravagances nearly bankrupted Rome and with support for him crumbling, Nero committed suicide in 68 CE.

Circus

There were no clowns at an ancient Roman circus, but plenty of action. Roman circuses were oval tracks where two-horse *biga* and four-horse *quadriga* chariots raced at lightning speeds. Races lasted for seven laps, cheered on by crowds of up to 150,000 people. Charioteers balanced on tiny wooden platforms between their chariot's wheels, shifting their body weight and pulling on the horses' reins to steer around corners. Crashes, injuries, and deaths from falls and tramplings were common, but successful survivors were richly rewarded; Gaius Appuleius Diocles won over 1,400 races and 9 million denarii, making him sport's first millionaire superstar.

Cena

For poor Romans, this main meal of the day might include bread, vegetables, porridge, and any meat they could afford. For the wealthy, it could be a multi-course feast eaten while reclining on couches in a dining room called the *triclinium*. The Romans didn't have forks and only used knives and spoons occasionally, so most food was eaten with fingers. Belching loudly showed appreciation of the cooking, and guests might slip food sneakily into their napkins to take home. A dinner banquet was a chance to impress with exotic dishes, from flamingo tongues and elephant's trunk to dormice in honey.

Pompeii

In 79 CE, disaster struck the prosperous Roman city of Pompeii on Italy's north-western coast. Vesuvius, a neighboring volcano, erupted for the first time in 1,800 years and showered the city with large stones and vast amounts of hot gases and ash. Many people fled but thousands were killed by heat, suffocating fumes, or collapsing and burning buildings. The city was abandoned and forgotten about for almost 1,700 years until it was rediscovered and excavations began in 1748. A perfectly preserved time capsule of Roman city life was found, including many homes, shops, mosaics, and a majestic 20,000 seat open-air theater.

Hadrian

Born in Spain, Hadrian (76–138 CE) was brought up by his father's cousin who became Emperor Trajan. Hadrian succeeded him in 117 CE and ruled peacefully for the next 21 years, over half of which was spent away from Rome, touring the empire. Seeking to defend the borders of Rome's territory, he built fortified walls called *limites* in Germany and northern England—the 73-mile-long Hadrian's Wall. An admirer of Greek culture and architecture, Hadrian had many grand structures built in Athens and Rome, including the Pantheon. He also sparked a fashion craze as the first emperor to have a full beard.

Calendar

Many peoples used the Moon to measure time. The Egyptians were the first to base their calendar on the Sun with three 120-day-long seasons and five "spare" days. The first Roman calendar had just 304 days, split into 10 months. New calendars were introduced in Rome, but they were out of sync with the seasons. To get calendars back on track, Julius Caesar insisted on 46BCE lasting 445 days. From then on, his calendar lasted 365¼ days, starting with January, named after Janus, the two-faced god of beginnings. An extra day was added once every four years—a leap year.

Praegustator

Imperial Rome was full of intrigue, secrecy, and evil plots, many involving poisoning, so it was no surprise that powerful and wealthy people often hired protection. As well as bodyguards, some Romans, especially emperors, would employ a slave as a praegustator—a food taster. The praegustator would taste all their employer's meals beforehand to ensure they weren't poisoned. One praegustator, though, is thought to have turned murderer in 54 CE by secretly feeding the Emperor Claudius some poisoned mushrooms. It is believed he was acting on the orders of Claudius' own wife, Agrippina, whose son, Nero, became emperor after Claudius' death.

Attila

This ruthless and feared leader of the wandering Hun tribes came to power
along with his brother, Bleda, in 434 CE. The Huns built a fearsome horseback army,
including members of other barbarian tribes such as the Goths. They made four major attacks
on Roman territory. The first, between 442 and 447 CE, in Eastern Europe, was followed by
invasions of Gaul (France) in 451 CE and Italy the following year. Attila is thought to have
murdered his brother around 445 CE to become sole leader of the Huns and took
huge amounts of gold as protection from the cities and empires he terrorized.

Barbarians

First used by Greeks to describe non-Greek speakers, the Romans used the word "barbarians" for many different tribes on the edges of their empire. These included the Huns, Franks, Goths, Visigoths, and Vandals. Roman armies battled barbarians successfully...at first. But from the 400s onward, barbarians from northern and eastern Europe invaded Rome's empire. The Vandals took over northern Africa and areas in Spain, while the Franks occupied parts of Gaul. In 410 CE, Rome was invaded for the first time in 800 years, by the Visigoths, led by Alaric I. Further attacks came before Rome finally fell in the 470s.

Graffiti

Whether you think of it as art or vandalism, graffiti is not a modern invention.
Instead of spray paint or permanent markers, ancient people used knives and sharp points
to carve words and drawings into stone walls and columns. Some ancient graffiti were
political statements, love poems, or even "I was here" type messages. Gossip and harsh words
about others were common, such as *Rusticus est Cordyon*, meaning "Rusticus is a clown,"
which was found in the Roman city of Pompeii. Some Romans went further, drawing rude
pictures and carving graffiti in the tomb of ancient Egyptian pharaoh Ramesses IV.

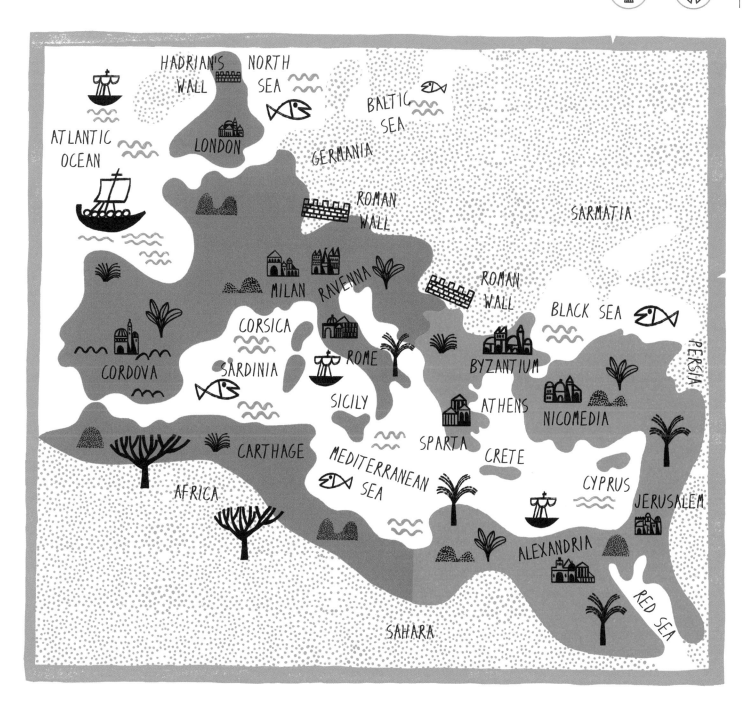

Byzantium

This glittering city and gateway between Europe and Asia boasted an important location next to the waters that linked the Mediterranean and Black Sea. It was controlled by Greeks, Spartans, and Persians at different times before coming under Roman rule. In 330 CE, the Roman emperor Constantine made it the new capital of the Roman Empire, renaming it Constantinople after himself. When the empire split into east and west, the city became the center of the eastern portion known as the Byzantine Empire. While the western Roman empire fell in the 470s, the Byzantine Empire thrived for almost another 1,000 years.

AUTHOR'S NOTE

Well, there you have it, 100 words about 100 people, places, gods, myths, ideas, objects, and events that helped make the ancient world what it was—a truly amazing place. These ancient civilizations dazzled the planet with their breathtaking art, architecture, ideas, and innovations. They not only had a massive impact at the time, but continue to do so to this very day. I hope you found these 100 topics as interesting to read as I found them to write. I am now utterly fascinated by mummies, triremes, Archimedes, and Hatshepsut. I don't fancy being a gladiator but I'd quite like to be a pharaoh. What about you? What were your favorites? Which ones were you surprised by? If, like me, this book leaves you with a thirst to know more, there are plenty of great museums, libraries, and online resources to really delve deeper into the amazing ancient world.

Happy reading!

Clive Gifford

TIMELINE

around 4000 BCE
Farming using channels that carry water from the Nile is used in ancient Egypt.

around 3500 BCE
The first hieroglyphs are painted on ancient Egyptian wall art.

3100 BCE
The upper and lower kingdoms of Egypt are united by King Menes.

2560 BCE
The Great Pyramid at Giza is built for the Egyptian pharaoh Khufu. It was the tallest building in the world for over 3,000 years.

around 2500 BCE
The Phoenicians make trade links with the ancient Egyptians.

around 1900 BCE
The Minoan civilization entered its peak period, beginning to build palaces and other impressive structures on the island of Crete.

around 1479 BCE
Hatshepsut becomes the first female ruler of ancient Egypt.

1327 BCE
Egyptian pharaoh Tutankhamun dies and is buried in a tomb that was rediscovered in 1922.

814 BCE

The city of Carthage is founded by the Phoenicians.

776 BCE

The date given for the first ancient Greek Olympic Games.

594 BCE

Solon gives Athenian citizens the vote, paving the way for the start of democracy in 508 BCE.

431–404 BCE

Sparta defeat Athens in the Peloponnesian War.

around 400 BCE

The ancient Greeks invent catapults for use in warfare.

323 BCE

Macedonian general Alexander the Great dies.

312 BCE

The first part of the Appian Way (the first major Roman road) is built, running south out of Rome.

241 BCE

The Romans capture Sicily, making it their first overseas territory.

149–146 BCE

The Third Punic Wars end and the Romans destroy Carthage.

73–71 BCE

Spartacus leads a rebellion of slaves against the Romans.

45 BCE

Julius Caesar introduces a new calendar.

31 BCE

Mark Antony and Cleopatra's armies are defeated at the Battle of Actium. Egypt became part of the Roman Empire shortly after.

31 BCE

Augustus (formerly Octavian) becomes ruler of Rome, later becoming the first emperor of Rome in 27 BCE.

79 CE

Pompeii is destroyed by volcanic eruptions.

80 CE

The Colosseum is opened in Rome.

117 CE

Under Emperor Trajan, the Roman Empire reaches its largest extent, home to almost a fifth of the entire world's population.

284 CE

Emperor Diocletian splits the Roman Empire in half for the first time. Emperor Constantine later reunited the empire in the 330s CE.

383–410 CE

Roman army legions leave Britain and Gaul (France).

395 CE

The Roman Empire is split in half again, with the western half ruled from Rome and the eastern half ruled from Constantinople (now Istanbul).

410 CE

Rome is invaded for the first time in 800 years by the Visigoths, led by Alaric I.

455 CE

Vandals invade Italy from Africa and attack Rome.

476 CE

The last emperor of the western Roman Empire is overthrown by Barbarians. The eastern Roman Empire (the Byzantine Empire) continued until 1453 CE.

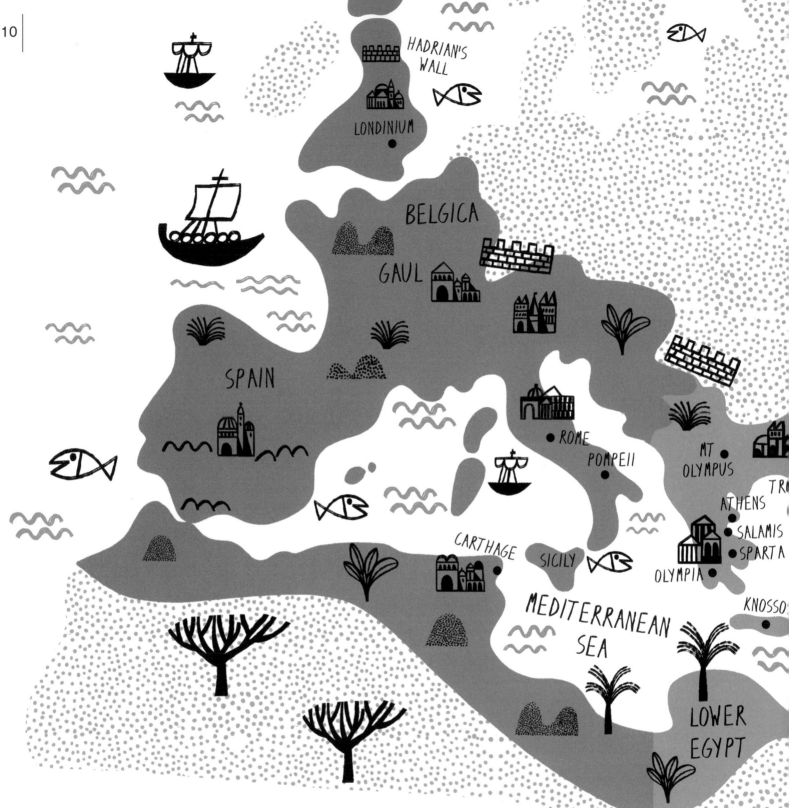

HADRIAN'S WALL

LONDINIUM

BELGICA

GAUL

SPAIN

ROME

POMPEII

MT OLYMPUS

TR

ATHENS

SALAMIS

SPARTA

CARTHAGE

SICILY

OLYMPIA

KNOSSO

MEDITERRANEAN SEA

LOWER EGYPT

ANCIENT WORLD MAP

The classical ancient world was centered around the regions of southern Europe, North Africa, and the Middle East. This map shows many of the key cities, islands, and places found in the ancient world. Explore the map to see where people lived and key events mentioned in this book took place.